I0654319

A GIRL &THE WEATHER

Prose and Poems

by

STEFAN ZWEIG

translated & with an afterword by William Ruleman

CEDAR SPRINGS BOOKS

Published by Cedar Springs Books, 2014, 2018.

ISBN-13: 978-0692327210
ISBN-10: 0692327215

Acknowledgments

The translator would like to express his gratitude to Lindi Preuss of Williams Verlag in Zürich for patiently corresponding with him and letting him know that the works in this book are now in the public domain. He is also grateful to Trudy Miller for reading the translations and making suggestions; to his daughter, Anne Ruleman Barach, for her patient care in preparing the manuscript for publication; and to the editors of the following journals, in which several of the pieces in this book first appeared:

The New English Review for "Nights on Lake Como," "The Hermit," and "Landscape."

Tears in the Fence for "A Girl and the Weather."

Open Writing for "Sunrise in Venice."

The Sonnet Scroll for "Autumn Sonnet."

CONTENTS

A NEW ABUNDANCE

O what glowing in strange new form
When my lips clung to yours. It's true:
Already I felt new richness warm
My soul as I went home from you.

So, all my longing lost in her,
I gave myself to infinity;
And heart and night and star now stir
With the selfsame melody.

DESIRE

On many days I'm seized by a deep desire
For joy and splendor, wild rhythms' glow, the bud
Of roses as dark and crimson in hue as blood—
For lustful women with lips of stormy fire,
For love to stem the tide of my craving's flood.

Yet deep in my every dazzling pleasure pang,
A single trembling wish alone will run
Toward realms where a richer happiness is won,
Domains where still and peaceful melodies sang
To me in childhood's ever golden sun.

AN URGE . . .

A trembling fills my heart, an urging towards
Some great and blessing happening—towards
A love that fills and swells, expands the soul
And holds each strange, stray stirring in its control.

I wait for hours, days, week after week;
My heart stays mute with words I cannot speak;
In weary songs, my longing disappears;
The heat of sultry nights drinks up my tears.

CARESSES

I love those first caresses, fraught with fears—
The ones that still half-question, half-confide—
Because, beyond them, wilder hours stride
And lodge themselves in life like massive piers.

A scent of blood's most fugitive sensation;
A smile, a passing glance, a tender hand;
They ever crackle, red sparks of temptation,
To fall in bursts within the night's firebrand.

Strangely sweet (for they are dealt in jest),
They still are mild, sans aim, confusion-kissed
Like trees, which, shaken by spring's raging zest,
Will shatter in the wind's rough fist.

THE DISTANT LANDSCAPE

It's just a dream I once dreamed long ago
When young or saw, perhaps, within a trance
On travels long forgotten since, although

Its image flashes now as if a lance
Of steel had ripped it clean from night's dark ground:
A lush and bright and lovely vale's expanse

That plunges down from mountains all around
As if to drink from streams that shock the air cold,
That smash against the rocks with crashing sound

And roll on, glittering, past a distant fold
Where ripe grapes' shadowy and velvet blue
Meanders down in gentle tracts of gold.

I see it clearly, yes: the picture's true:
In every dream, the same old steep roof ridges,
Warm with sun. I breathe deep, take my cue

From sultry southern air, hear from the bridge's
Dizzying height the waters foam and then
Descry a white path spinning along both edges.

And questions stir and urge me on again:
Have I roamed this way before? If yes,
Was it life or dream? And where? And when?

The white path with its timid *S*
Conveys the crags' smoke on down through the vale,
From where—and *where* to— I can only guess;

It shimmers through my nights, an opal veil
That fills me, brimming, longing, to go on
That path, and far beyond the dale

To a land that lies past every dream, a zone
Quite dim and distant yet serene, ablaze
With clouds: a land as strange yet strangely well-known

To me as my own childhood's days.

EVENING SOUNDS

A sound of singing's on the air
So full of mild and longing ring
As if, on the silent wood-seam there—
Cheeks pale, tears clouding over his stare—
Stood the suffering little son of the king.

And, through lily-tender hands,
He scans, despite the blazing light,
The crimson vista he commands
Of Love's way home from distant lands,
Although his love's nowhere in sight.

HYMN FOR THE JOURNEY

Blue veins of ice appear to groove
A rushing web through distant lands.
Flow with them, heart! Get up and *move*.
Flight alone can free you from law-and-might's bands.

Flight alone can free you from habit's millstone,
Which binds and crushes your one true self.
Plunge into the vast and blank unknown;
Only distant lands can win back that old self!

See! But a tug, and already in flight!
It beats for you there: an iron breast;
Home falls back with each slope and height.
New sights remind you that you are blessed.

They fade, the borders and their stations;
Strange tongues unite you to the soul
Of endless union embracing the nations—
The fourteen folk—in Europe's whole.

And in the flourishing of the far,
Your soul awakes; your gaze now clears;
The world, in a dance from star to star,
Rests in the music of the spheres.

THE STILFSERJOCH-STRASSE

The train's only now leaving Landeck, but it's not on a real mountain journey yet. The black and yellow mail coach moves at a leisurely trot; again and again, we take on board the dust-coated packs of mountain hunters who take their maneuvers here; and the lively boys, with their sun-burned faces, climb into the wagon laughing.

Yet by and by, the mountains squeeze together and press the Inn, which foams an ashen gray, down into a narrow bed. They're shoved ever closer together; even the road has no more room: three or four times, it springs from the right shore to the left, gets pushed out of the way more and more, and finally clambers anxiously round a bend and on up the rocks, scattering them in a few spots.

After a couple of hours, we're in Finstermünz, and already a thousand meters up. And it feels like it from the view, even if the gray mountain massif still hems us in all around. For to the Inn, which earlier babbled along past the road, there is now a path: a long, laborious descent through green firs and meadows to the bank: a steep, one-half-hour's journey in a romantic valley of crags.

But the excursion rewards. At last we reach an ancient four-cornered tower that stands in the middle of the Inn above the bridge that leads to both shores, so we can expect a pleasant surprise. Here we stride across the bridge through the tower, with its open gate painted yellow and black, and stand astonished over a little sign with the word *Switzerland*. In half an hour, we've unexpectedly taken a cheap little trip from Finstermünz to that country. Now we also know that the distant mountaintops (whose gleam of snow, unfortunately, blurs again and again with the dun-colored fog of the unfriendly day) are the mountains of the Engadine. We gladly trudge our way up the serpentine path to

Finstermünz and the road again, and there the packs of mountains are, once more, only dustier and also ever more resistant. They move on, but we spend the night—a starless, lackluster night—in Finstermünz.

In the morning, the fog still lingers round the window like the veils of giant princesses; and the mountains loom in the mist. But we risk the journey back. The wagon rushes past the threatening fortress of Nauders, leaves the Inn Valley and with it, for a while, the threatening walls of rock. On past the pretty village of Reschen and the desolate deep-green lake: the most famous watershed between the Adriatic and Black Seas. In a steady drizzle, we finally reach Saint Valentine, where, for the very first time, the long-sought chain of the Ortlers begins to gleam. But it's only a *half-gleam*: white flecks of fog rest heavily round the peaks, and with only a fleeting greeting does one of the tall lords, at times, reveal himself. But now we know that all this is but a prelude.

Not till Neusponding—one of those pretty little Tirolean villages with nothing to say—does the actual Stilfserjoch-strasse begin. We get there late in the afternoon, and the skies are starting to clear. In a broad, stony bed beside the road, the Trafoier brook crashes harshly about, shooting up a hard and icy spray that fills the air with a wonderful, snowy chill. Again, the path gets laborious; the horses move in a heavy, slow trot. The mountain masses lean dreadfully over the rising road, which, with its elegant, narrow white line, seems like something quite rash and foolhardy here in this world of giants, which is constantly filled with the thunder of rushing water. One feels an emotion somewhere between fear and awe in this silent world: that mild and reluctant emotion one feels only before the sublime, as Kant has defined it; but it's suddenly dissolved—almost in a heartbeat—in the pure emotion of admiration, for, as the road turns toward the heights, where Trafoi lies, a panorama of unforgettable beauty begins to gleam. The massif of Ortler and that of Mont Livrio, intertwined like sisters at heights that are incomprehensible, struggle their way out of a now quite tender fog, and the broad white expanse of a shiny world of glaciers miraculously brightens the landscape. And already one sees, set in the beautiful profile of this alpine world, the tiny, quite tiny valley of Trafoi and its pretty hotel, whose banners appear to be waving. One gets closer without even noticing it, for the glaciers and the heights, from which water plunges down in wild and almost desperate leaps; the spray of the brook, which struggles its way out of the bridges of ice; the broad stream of boulders, which speak of colossal winter avalanches; the strange and almost venomous green of the moraine; and even the sky, that close sky with its chasing clouds, which only seems to stretch from peak to peak—all of it has no equal in terms of the grandeur of its sudden manifestation.

We spend the night in the smart and spruce Hotel Trafoi. But the next day it seems that we're already getting alarmingly close to two thousand meters, and even the sluggish but steadily forward-moving trot of the wagon seems too fast. Or is it only at such heights that, in many people, the tourist's soul first awakes? Does it first, as the plants need the sun, need the glaciers and masses of moraine? We march on foot. On and on. The magnificent Stilfserjoch-strasse, ascending the enormous heights in zigzag windings that, at the same time, are smooth and well-tended as a trotting course, seems too easy: we choose a complex system of stairs—just to be able to admire this wonderful stretch of road, which clambers, smooth and white, up the mountains like bright smoke. Already, at the white knot of a stone pyramid that proudly peers down into the Trafoi

16

Valley, a strange thing happens to us: a total change as to what we feel is of worth. Trafoi, which we admired yesterday in our climb and arrival as a bright destination, is forgotten, lost: a poor little point in the deep, deep valley that seems screwed into these huge masses as if by a giant spinning top. The distant expanses, which, from the lowlands, resembled white sparks at first, then bright cloths that from far away almost ever appear to wave in the sky, are close, quite close; and giants like the Ortler and the Madatsch, which yesterday were still towers in the sky, are reachable today, almost friends—indeed, almost powerful companions to whom one could devote oneself. And they actually come close as one climbs higher; snow—snow incarnate—lies on the road; and the broad streams of ice are only steps from the pass. Along with it, the road (this Austrian work of art), spins on as if it were passing through colorful meadows; cars chuff their way up at a leisurely pace; the post drives on with its bright little ringing. The panorama turns grandiose: left and right, more and more white mountains arise; for a long time now, the trees have ceased to appear; even the last green has faded. At the height of the pass, at the hotel, is the border: the Dreisprachenspitze, or "three-language peak." One can light a cigarette at the hotel door, walk from Austria to Italy, from Italy to Switzerland, from Switzerland back to Italy, and the stub's still burning—anyhow, a nice little joke at 2,800 meters high. Here the vista grows in boundlessness, yet one's eyes can hardly tolerate the thinness of the air. Even so, the chorus of blessed boys from *Faust* comes to mind:

> That is powerful to behold,
> And yet the sight is too gloomy.

One almost stumbles about in its smoke. We're glad to climb onto the road again, but now it's toward Italy. Just a few steps, and we're at the bordering canton, and the first beggars instruct us, with their mere presence, that we're in Italy already. The sweeping snake of road keeps winding on ("The road the Austrians built for us," the Italians here say in triumph) down in a splendid serpentine. And, as if at the very border that bright world would already start, the sky begins to shine a gentian blue, and the clouds are whiter and roam more tenderly. As the road sinks, the view comes to life. A unique and full, lush green spins over the fields: that bright, miraculous Alpine green of Segantini's pictures, and already one feels that air one thinks he can taste in those pictures: that pure air of endless mountain meadows, snow-chill and spiced with the scents of Alpine blooms. The mountains are no less high, yet they lean more kindly down into the valley. Huts dare to rest on them. The road zigzags more and more, breaks through the rocks in several tunnels wherein the water drops black and cold, and moves along with the Braulio, which springs incessantly, from rock to rock, like a colt, down to Adda. And it's the event of a lifetime how the road, still more than a thousand meters high, turns suddenly; and the deep green valley of Bormio, already flecked throughout with glittering wheat, lights up for one: such a soft and mild and wonderful view that one will never forget it, all of sweet Italy, bordered by a chain of tall, snowy mountains. Slowly, quite slowly, with hesitant steps, one descends into the valley, which almost does not lie any deeper than Trafoi. But here roses shine; dark trees twine tenderly round the rocks. And now the road no longer gleams boldly, defiantly, as it did in the Tirol: instead, it will entice one mildly and tenderly into the Veltliner Valley, where the fine, large, and dark grapes glow; and the wonderful wine of Italy sparkles in the sun as crimson as hot blood.

NIGHT ON A MOUNTAIN LAKE

My light boat drifts in waves whose pallid tints
The rings of stars reflect in sparkling dream.
And streams of silver sheathed in fragrant scents
Leap from the hills laved in the moon's kind gleam.

In heavy folds and drapes and cloaks of light,
Tired mist sinks down amid the lakeshore trees;
The pines all round are staring, dark with spite,
Like calcified and care-worn reveries.

The night sows peace abroad with gentle hand
And hovers tenderly amid the throng
Of wildly-jagged walls of rock that stand
Above my shiny bark, which rocks along

Sans sound as lake water laps and splashes
Silently against the blond lumber.
Deep calm . . . Yet distant lightning flashes
Like thoughts awakened from dark slumber.

NIGHTS ON LAKE COMO

What do you take from these starry nights—
O heart, in all your disarray?
Yes, what do you take from their delights
To guide you on your path by day?

What did you feel when, in the pale
Pond's shell, its silver overswelled;
When, deep within the resting vale,
A trembling stream of starlight welled?

Can it slip into shadow, as over the ring
Of hills, a white flash passed (night's noon),
And, as the rushing bluish wing
Of a cloud clung round the moon?

Can it shatter, like the silent blooms
That softly waft their heated prayer
Over the rich villas' doors and rooms
To your breathing heart in the late-night air?

Can it quiver too, as, softer, lighter,
(A sinking string of pearls or lace),
The moon's gleam over the rocking water
Fled for the dark without a trace?

Is nothing left of the whispering spray
Of the cypresses along the shore,
Not one of your dream thoughts that would stray
Along your round for an hour or more?

Perhaps but a verse of the wind in its reeling
And pure longing for that time that could bless

Like fragrance lost in a gentle feeling
Of inexpressible tenderness.

IN BLOOM

Girls in spring's first glorious days—
So light and wonderful and fair.
They drift forth in a silent daze
Oblivious of, like crowns ablaze,
The flowers in their hair.

They wander toward the wind's violin—
A prayerful primaveral choir—
And languid longing deep within
Pinks their dreamy pallid skin
With many a florid fire.

And everything that vaguely strives
Wins in them a deeper meaning,
For everything within their lives
Contains earth's quivering raptures, thrives
Upon the thrill of spring's chill greening.

A GIRL AND THE WEATHER

It was hot that summer—so hot that, for years afterwards, we still cringed when we thought of the drought that had ruined the crops all over. As early as June and July, in fact, the fields were already parched with thirst. Yes, a few feeble showers still teased them then, but ever since August had rolled around, not a single drop had fallen; and even up here, in the Tyrol's high valleys, where I'd hoped (like everyone else, it seemed) to find some cool air for a change, the sky glowed crimson with dust and fire.

By early morning, the sun—as sallow and dull as the eye of somebody sick with a fever—already glared from the blank sky onto the panting earth; and, as it climbed through the day, a heavy white steam flowed little by little from noon's brassy cauldron to blanket the valley in haze. Of course, you could see, far off, the Dolomites, mighty and free: snow gleamed from them, clean and clear. But your eyes alone felt this shimmer of chill—in a way that stuck in your craw. It hurt you to gaze at them soulfully, to think of the winds that maybe, right at that moment, roared and rushed all around them while here, in the cauldron, a greedy warmth pressed down night and day, sucking up all your bodily moisture like so many tiny lips.

All that lived in this withering world of wilting plants, languishing leaves, and shriveling brooks was dying, bit by bit. The hours grew idle and sluggish. Like everyone else, I mainly spent those endless days alone in my room, half-nude, with the window blinds drawn. Yes, I just whiled my time away—in a dazed and helpless dream, a weak-willed vigil for some sort of change, for some cool air again—for some good thunderstorms, some *rain*. But soon all these wishes shrank to a brooding as stupid and helpless as that of the drooping grass and the sultry dream of the brittle and steamy woods.

It just grew hotter from day to day. And still the rain wouldn't come. From dawn to dusk, the sun burned low. By and by, her pained and sallow face assumed the dull stare of a lunatic. All of life, it seemed, had come to a halt; for everything stood still. The animals made no more noises. Not a sound came forth from the parched white fields but the gentle singing of vibrating heat, the seething of the boiling world. I longed to go out, to go into the woods, where blue shadows quivered between the trees—to lie there eluding the sun's dogged stare; but even these few steps were too much for me. So I stayed crouched down in a wicker chair in the hotel entry for an hour or two—all slumped down in the narrow shadows that the shielding roof edge stretched on the gravel.

Once I moved farther out than the area cut by the thin, four-cornered shadow. The sun crept over my hand. Then I leaned back, brooding stupidly in the stupid light— without wish or will or sense of time. In fact, time melted in this awful mugginess. The hours were cooked to a pulp: dissolved in hot and senseless daydreams. On my flesh, I felt only the air as it rushed and burned its way into my pores; within, my blood throbbed with a feverish, frantic hammer's beat.

Then nature seemed to *breathe*, with a soft and longing breath. A hot, yearning sigh seemed to rise from somewhere. I drew myself up. Wasn't that the *wind?* I'd almost forgotten what it was like. My withered lungs hadn't drunk such coolness for way too long. Yet I hadn't even realized that till it whisked up and hit me right in the face—right there in my spot of feeble roof shadow. But those trees across the slope must have sensed some strange presence, for at once they started, very gently, to sway. They seemed to bow and

24

whisper to one another. The shadows between them were restless. Like something alive and excited, they flitted here and there.

Then at once they lifted, somewhere far off, with a deeper, more vibrating sound. I mean it. *Wind* came over the world: a whispering, whining, and spinning—a deep and thundering roaring—then a stronger, mightier thrust. Like someone suddenly frightened by something, dust clouds like smoke now whirled through the streets, each toward the same unknown destination. The birds, who'd been resting somewhere in the dark, now whizzed past, black in the air. The horses' nostrils snuffled froth, and way off in the valley, the cows mooed. Some violent thing had woken up; it must be close by. The earth knew. So did the animals and trees. A light gray veil sailed across the sky.

I shook with agitation. Heat prickled and vexed my blood. My nerves crackled, grew tight. I'd never yearned so keenly—so *much*—for all the voluptuousness of the wind, the blissful joy of a thunderstorm. And it was coming! It was on its way! It seemed to swell and *announce* itself. The wind was nudging soft tangles of cloud across the sky. It was gasping and snorting behind the mountains, like someone rolling some massive load.

At times these snorting, gasping shoves seemed to get tired and die down. And then the firs, like eavesdropping meddlers, slowly quivered, grew still. My heart quivered right along with them. Everywhere I looked, I saw the same hushed waiting I felt inside. The earth had stretched her pores—torn them open—like tiny and thirsty mouths. I felt it in my own body too, which seemed to open pore by pore—to stretch, expand with a craving for coolness, for the shuddering thrill of cool rain. My fingers clenched as if by instinct—as if they wanted to clutch those clouds and drag them down into the wilting world.

But they were coming—as if they'd been shoved by some unseen hand. They were dark and sluggish—round, thick, black sacks burdened down with *rain*—and they blustered and grumbled like solid things as they jostled one another. At times a soft wind, like a crackling match, sputtered over their black expanse. Then they flared up, blue and dangerous, grew thicker and thicker and waxed even blacker in their own richness, forcing themselves ever on. Like a theater's curtain or a lump of lead, the sky kept sinking down. Now blackness devoured it; the warm, choked air congealed; one last expectant pause set in, awful and mute. As it sank down over the valley, the black weight seemed to choke everything: the birds no longer chirped; the trees stood holding their breaths; even the grass blades didn't dare tremble. The sky was like a metal coffin that sealed inside it the whole hot world, with everything trapped within waiting numbly for the first lightning flash.

I stood there clasping my hands, unable to breathe. My nerves were strained in a sweet and wonderful angst that froze me rigid. Behind me, people were rushing around, fleeing the woods, scrambling in through the hotel door. The servant girls slammed the shutters, drew down the windows with a crash. Everyone was active, excited— stirring, bustling, getting *ready*. I was the only one standing still. I felt all giddy and feverish—all bottled up for that shout I could feel deep down in my throat: the shriek of joy I'd emit with the first lightning flash.

Then suddenly, right behind me, a sigh. That's it: a *sigh*. It came from a tortured breast, and with it, these words—words of begging, longing, and agony:

"If it would just *rain*!"

And it was so wild, so *primal*, this voice—this thrust from some stifled emotion. To me it seemed that the earth

26

itself—all parched and pained and suffocating—had screamed aloud with its wide open lips.

I turned round. Behind me stood a girl. And she was the one who must have said the words, for her own lips (pale, softly quivering), were open as if from thirst. She was gripping the door and trembling. She'd not spoken to me or to anyone. She leaned toward the view as if over a cliff; she stared with a blank look into that darkness hovering over the firs. It was black and empty, this look—glassy, as if from a bottomless depth against the deep sky. It pierced deep into the mass of clouds, into the brooding thunderstorm, with a kind of greed, and it wasn't aware of me at all.

So I could observe her without her noticing me, this stranger completely oblivious of me, and I saw, as her breast rose, how something choking shuddered above it, as now, around her throat, a tender yet bony spot detached itself from her dress and a shiver went up, till her lips quivered too—opened thirstily—and she said, again:

"If it would just *rain*."

And this was the sigh of the whole sultry world for me. There was something incredible about the figure she cut there, all statuesque and relaxed in her pose and yet like a sleepwalker too. And as she lingered there, stark white in her flimsy dress against that lead sky, she seemed one with all nature's yearning thirst.

Something hissed in the grass beside me. Something pecked hard at the ledge. Something crunched in the gravel. All over, at once, stirred this soft, buzzing sound . . . Then I knew. I felt it. These drops, falling hard, were the first steaming spears, the blessèd heralds of the great and rushing cool rain! Oh, it had begun! A kind of oblivion came over me: a drunken ecstasy. I felt more alert than I had in my life.

Leaping forward, I captured a drop in my palm. It clapped hard and cold on my flesh. I tore off my cap—to feel more acutely the wet delight on my hair and brow. I quivered impatiently to let the rain rush all around me completely, to feel it upon me, all over my warm and crackling skin, in the open pores—on, on till deep in my vexed, heated blood. They were still sparse, yes, those splashing drops, but already I felt their rich descent; already I heard them streaming and rushing, the opened sluices; already I felt the sky crashing down with blessing bliss, down into the forests, down into the whole sultry, burning world.

But it was strange. The drops wouldn't fall any faster. You could count them: One, two, three as they fell, each crackling, hissing, whistling gently right and left . . . But they wouldn't combine with the others to make that good old crashing and rushing music of *rain*. They just dropped down timidly. And instead of accelerating, the rhythm just grew slower and slower.

Then at once it ceased—as an old clock will do when it croaks and time itself appears to stand still. My heart had been pounding impatiently, but now it seemed to stop, grow cold. I waited. But nothing happened. Black and rigid, the sky stared down with darkened brow; for minutes on end, it stayed dead still; then only a soft, scornful light seemed to flit across its face. In the west, the heights brightened; by and by, the wall of clouds dissolved; crashing gently, they rolled farther on. More and more, they lost their depthless look. In unconscious, unfulfilled disappointment, the listening landscape lay beneath the glistening horizon. One last soft and raging shaking ran through the trees, which bent and buckled. Then the hands of the leaves, which had stretched back greedily, fell limply, as if they were dead. The veil of clouds thinned; an angry and dangerous brightness loomed over the helpless and impotent world. Nothing had happened: the storm had just *left*.

My whole body shook. Fury was what I felt: the indignation of senseless impotence, the utter letdown of betrayal. I could have screamed and raved! A longing to smash something rose up in me, a desire for evil and danger: a senseless need for revenge. I felt in me all the torment of nature, completely betrayed: the prickly glow of the limestone, the pant of the tiny grass blades, the heat of the streets, the smoke of the woods—the thirst of the totally cheated world. My nerves burned like wires: I felt them flash from the charged and electric tension in the air. They blazed like fine flames beneath my skin, which seemed stretched tight.

Everything gave me agony. Every sound had points. Tiny flames seemed to circle everything, and all that I seized with my stare looked seared. I was agitated to the depths of my being; senses that usually slept still and dead in my musty brain had opened like so many delicate nostrils, each of which burned, it seemed. I could hardly tell my own mood from the world's: the thin membrane between me and it was torn. Everything stirred with an odd kindred feeling—a strange and mutual disappointment—and staring feverishly into the valley, which little by little filled with lights, I felt that each one flickered inside me, that each star burned right into my blood.

The same feverish fervor seemed everywhere, both inside and outside me too. With a painful enchantment, I felt that everything welling up around me was forcing itself into *me*—growing, glowing there. The mysterious core of life, which preserves all variety in a single thing, seemed to sizzle, and from deep within, with a magic alertness of sense, I felt everything: the rage of each leaf; the dull gaze of the dogs, who slunk round the doors with drooping tails; yes, I felt it all, and all that I felt gave me pain. This blaze began to swell in me almost bodily, and as my fingers touched the door, the wood crackled beneath them like hot, dry tinder.

The gong sounded for the evening meal. Its coppery clang—which was also painful—struck deep into me. I turned round. Where were the people who'd rushed past earlier, all agitated and anxious? Where was the girl who'd stood like the craving world—the one who, in all my confusion and disappointment, I'd completely forgotten? They'd all vanished. I stood alone with the silence of nature.

I turned again to the far-off heights. The sky was perfectly empty now, but not clear. A strained and greenish haze lay over the stars, and the rising moon glittered with the evil gloss of a cat's eyes. All above me was wan, mocking, dangerous; but deep beneath this uncertain sphere, night dawned, dark as a tropical sea, phosphorescent, and with the agonized, yearning breath of a woman: one who has known disappointment.

Overhead, still bright and scornful, one last bright spot glowed under a tired and oppressive, muggy darkness; each was hostile to the other in this still, eerie struggle of sky and earth. I breathed deeply but drank in nothing but irritation. Then I reached down into the grass. It was blue, dry as timber, and it crackled blue in my fingers.

The gong called again. Its dead sound repulsed me. I wasn't hungry, I felt no longing for other people, but this sultry solitude was too dreary. The whole heavy sky weighed down on my breast in leaden silence, and I felt I could bear its pressure no longer, so I went on into the dining hall.

People were already seated at their little tables, chatting gently; and yet, for me, this chatter was way too loud. For me everything—the lisping of lips, the clink of utensils, the rattling of plates—was torture, torment, a scraping away at my frayed, feeble nerves. Each gesture, each breath, each look flashed before me and gave me pain. I had to force myself not to do something senseless, for I could feel it in my pulse: all my senses had fever. I had to look at each of these people, and toward every last one, I felt nothing but hate. As I watched them sitting so peacefully— so gluttonous and leisurely—I glowered. I envied them for the way they could rest so satisfied and sure in themselves, not sharing at all in the world's agony, not feeling at all the silent frenzy that stirred in the breast of the thirsting earth.

I fixed them all with my stare. Wasn't there someone who felt as the earth did? They all seemed so dull and uncaring. They were the ones who could rest, breathe, and take their leisure. They were the alert and healthy ones—but also the insensitive. I was the only sick one—the only one with the world's craving fever.

When the waiter brought my food, I tried a bit, but could not get it down, for all that I tasted or touched repelled me. I was much too full of the muggy haze, the foul-smelling vapor of suffering, sick, and tormented nature.

And then, when, near me, a chair rocked, I gave a start, for every sound stung me now like hot ice. Some strangers were sitting there—new neighbors I didn't know yet— an elderly man and his wife: calm bourgeois people with round, composed eyes and ruminant, "chewing" cheeks. But across from them, half with her back to me, sat a young girl: their daughter, I guessed.

She sat nearly motionless there. At first I saw just her neck, slim and white, and over it, like a steel helmet, her full head of black, almost bluish hair. But then, in her stare, I saw it. She was the same girl I'd seen on the terrace earlier, the one craving rain, like some open and thirsting white bloom. Her little fingers were sickly and slim. They fidgeted with her knife and fork, but (luckily for me) without clinking them; and this silence about her did me good. And too, she touched not a bite, though once her hand reached hastily, greedily for her glass.

Oh, *she* felt it too: the world's fever! I sensed it in the greedy way she seized the glass in her thirst; and so, with a friendly sympathy, my gaze settled on her neck. Here, I felt, was one not wholly shut off from nature—one other soul who also glowed in the blaze of a world; and I wanted her to know it: here we were the same. I longed to cry out to her: "*I* feel too! *I'm* feeling it too! I'm *conscious* like you! I'm *suffering* like you! Look at *me*! *I feel!*"

My desire, in fact, was like some magnet that glowed. And so I embraced her with it. Stared into her back. Caressed her hair. Bored *into* it, from afar, with my stare. I even called out to her, miming with my lips. I pressed myself on her, stared and stared, hurled my whole fever toward her so she, like a sister, would feel it too—right along with me.

But she wouldn't turn round. She just sat there—stiff as a statue, cool and strange. Nobody helped me. She was just like the rest, didn't feel what I felt. The world was not in her either. I burned alone.

Oh, this sultriness outside and in! I couldn't bear it anymore. The steam of warm food, greasy and sweetish, tormented me; every noise drilled into my nerves. I felt my blood bubble—felt close to a faint. All inside me craved cool air and distant climes, and this closeness to people stifled, overwhelmed me.

Seeing a window nearby, I shoved it open—pushed it out wide. And wonderfully, there it was again, wholly mysterious, this restless flickering in my blood, only melted now in the night sky's endless depths. A whitish yellow shimmered over the moon, like an inflamed eye in a red ring of haze; and some pale and foul-smelling vapor crept over the fields like a ghost. The crickets chirped from thirst—screamed and shrilled with metal strings. The whole air seemed strained. Every now and then, softly, and making no sense, a toad croaked; dogs barked loudly, howled; somewhere far off, wild animals bellowed. Feverish nights like this, I recalled, could poison cows' milk. Nature was sick, and so was this silent frenzy of bitterness. Staring through that window was like staring into a mirror of my own emotions. My whole being leaned forward as I did. My own sultriness, and that of the landscape, flowed into each other in a still and damp embrace.

Again the easy chair near me moved. Again I gave a start. Dinner had ended; people were getting up noisily. My neighbors rose up and went past me: the father first, all leisurely and satisfied, with a friendly, smiling look; then the mother; and at last the daughter. Now, for the first time, I saw her face. It was sallow, pale, with the same dull, sickly hue as the moon outside. The lips were still, and half open as they'd been earlier. She went noiselessly, but not lightly. Something limp and dull lay within her that oddly reminded me of my own feeling. I felt her come closer, and I got excited. Something in me yearned for intimacy with her— maybe the way she brushed against me with her white dress, or the way I could feel her hair's fragrance in passing. Whatever the case, she then gave me a look that pierced right into me and stayed there, glassy and black, deep and absorbing, for me alone to feel. Above it, her bright face faded; and I felt this murky darkness in front of me, which I dropped into as if into a well. Though she stepped just a pace ahead, her stare wouldn't let me go, but, black and glassy, bored into me like a lance, piercing deeper and deeper till its point touched right at my heart and stood still and for one, two moments, she held her stare on me and I held my breath—moments in which I felt helpless to tear away from those pupils' black magnets. Then she walked on past. And right there and then I felt my blood gush out as if from a gash and stream excitedly all through my body.

Now what in the world . . . I woke like one from the land of the dead. Did my fever make me confused me like that—make me get so lost with her just walking past? No. It had been as though, in this look, I'd felt that same still frenzy, that same languishing, senseless, thirsting greed that had opened itself up to me in everything: the earth's parched lips, the red moon's gaze, the animals' shrieking agony—the same pain that flashed and trembled in *me*. Ah, how everything was getting all mixed up together in this sultry night, this *incredible* night of impatient expectation!

Was *I* insane? Or was the *world*? Agitated, wanting an answer, I followed her into the hall, where now she was sitting next to her parents, reclining quietly in an easy chair, the dangerous look invisible now beneath her downcast eyelids. She seemed to be reading a book, but she wasn't— not really. I was sure that, if she felt like me—if she suffered the sweltering world's senseless agony—then she couldn't just sit there resting and quietly contemplating, that all was a front concealing a strange curiosity. So I sat down across from her and stared at her, waiting feverishly for the gaze that had so bewitched me—to see if it wouldn't come back and solve its mystery for me.

But she would not stir. Her hand flipped leaf after leaf of the book, with casual indifference; her look remained overcast while I waited across from her there, waited more and more fervently, some puzzling force of will in me exerting itself, with muscular strength, to shatter this disguise. Among all the people there talking leisurely, smoking and playing cards, a silent struggle now commenced. I felt her refusal, her resistance to look up, but the more she resisted, the stronger my defiance willed it. And I was strong, for inside me burned all the longing of the panting earth, all the thirsting glow of the disappointed world. And so, as the night's mugginess pressed and pressed at my pores, so my will pressed at hers. Soon she would *have* to give me a look; she'd have to!

While, in the hall behind us, someone began to play the piano; while the sounds rippled lightly over to me (up and down in fleeting scales); while, right across from me, a party now laughed over some silly joke; I heard everything, I felt everything, without letting up for one minute. I counted aloud the seconds in which I pulled and, well, *sucked* at her eyelids with my stare—the seconds in which, from a distance, through a kind of hypnosis, I *willed* her to lift her stubborn, bowed head.

At last, after endless minutes had seemed to pass, and the sounds from across the hall had kept purling, and I could feel my strength starting to subside, all at once she rose with a jolt and looked at me—and me alone. It was, once again, that same *infinite* look: a dreadful, absorbing, black Nothingness: a thirst that sucked me in without my being able to resist. I stared into those pupils as if staring into the black hole of a camera lens, and I felt my face being hurled away from myself and pulled inside this stranger's blood. The floor vanished under my feet; I felt all the utter sweetness of giddy falling. High above me, the ringing scales still rolled up and down, but I no longer knew where I was. My blood was streaming away; my breath faltered. I felt it was choking me—this minute, hour, eternity . . . Then her eyelids shut again.

I shot back up like a drowning person from deep underwater: freezing, shaking from danger and fear.

Then I looked round. She was still over there across from me, right in the middle of everyone, quietly bending over her book, once again just a slender young girl— motionless, picturesque—only gently, beneath her thin skirt, one knee bobbed up and down. My hands trembled too. I knew that now, if this lascivious game of anticipation and resistance should re-commence, I'd have to summon several strained minutes in order to be plunged back into her stare's black flame. My temples were moist; my blood seethed in me.

I could bear it no longer. Without turning round, I stood up and went out.

The night lay before the shining inn. The valley seemed sunken. The sky shone as damp and black as wet moss. But no cool air out here—still none. Everywhere here, too, I felt the same dangerous mating of thirst and drunkenness that I felt in my blood. Something unhealthy, damp, like the smell of someone with a fever, lay over the fields; the milk-white steam rose up; distant fires flared and roamed through the heavy air; and around the moon lay a yellow ring that made its gaze look evil. I felt infinitely tired. Seeing a cane chair out there, left from the day, I threw myself into it. My limbs collapsed, and I sprawled there, motionless.

And only then, nestled there, yielding to the soft cane, did the sultriness suddenly seem marvelous. It no longer pained me; it just pressed down on me— tender and voluptuous—and I didn't fight it. I just held my eyes shut, trying to see nothing, trying to feel nature—the living nature embracing me—all the more strongly. While a soft and slippery and sucking essence, polyp-like, now pressed all around me; while the night grazed me with a thousand lips, I lay there and felt myself succumb, give way to whatever it was that embraced me, that surrounded me, and that my blood drank; and, for the first time, I felt in this sultry encirclement something sensual like a woman, something dissolved in the mild ecstasy of devotion. A sweet sort of horror it was, to be suddenly lacking the strength to resist, to give my whole body up to the world. It was wonderful to let something unseen gently stroke my skin, to let my joints loosen. I didn't resist this relaxing of sense. No, I let myself glide along in it, feeling dreamily, darkly, only this: that the night and that earlier image of the girl, distressed by the weather, were one, and that it was sweet to be lost in them. This darkness seemed to be her alone, and the warmth that touched my limbs, her own body, dissolved in the night like mine. In touch with her as if in a dream, I vanished in a warm, black wave of abandon.

Then something startled me. I gathered up all my wits, but I couldn't tell where I was. Then I saw that I'd leaned back and closed my eyes. I'd fallen asleep! I must have napped there an hour or more, for the light in the hotel hall was already out, and everything was quiet. My hair was moist; it stuck to my temples: this dreamless but dreamlike slumber seemed to have settled on me like some feverish dew.

Completely confused, I stood up to find my way back to the inn, feeling vague and dull, but then all this confusion surrounded me too. Far off, something bawled, and now and then sheet lightning flashed in the sky. The air tasted of fire and sparks. Behind the mountains, lightning glared quite treacherously; and inside me, memories and forebodings phosphoresced. I'd have liked to stay, to reflect, to savor it all—maybe even resolve this mysterious state of affairs—but the hour was late, so I went in.

The hall was already empty, I found. By some chance the easy chairs stood all backed up against one another in the pallid sheen of a single light. They looked like ghosts in their mute emptiness; and without meaning to, I placed in one the tender shape of the tender being who'd confused me so with her look. (Her image still lived deep inside me, you know.) Now it stirred, and I felt that it gleamed at me. In fact, I felt a strange premonition that she was still awake, still up somewhere within these walls, and the promise of that ignited my blood. And the air was still so sultry! I'd hardly shut my eyes before I could feel crimson sparks behind the lids. The white glowing day still gleamed in me, still worked feverishly in me even now in this shimmering, damp, and sparkling, incredible night.

But I couldn't stay here in the hall: it was all too dark and deserted. So I went up the steps, though I didn't want to. Some rebellious streak remained in me—one that I didn't quite want to tame. I was tired, yet it seemed too early to go to sleep. Some mysterious, subtly addictive scent still promised something bizarre for me, and there on the staircase, my senses strained to catch sight of something alive and warm, pressed forth from me like so many fine and supple feelers that brushed against every bedchamber. As earlier, outside in nature, I now hurled my whole feeling into the house and felt the leisurely breathing of everyone sleeping therein: the heavy and dreamless surging of all their thick black blood, their simple peace and stillness, yet also the magnetic pull of some unknown power. I sensed that something in here was just as awake as I was.

Was it the thought of her, or was it the weather, that had formed this fine purple passion in me? I seemed to feel something through rampart and wall; a little flame of unrest quivered in me, enticed my blood, and would not burn out. Reluctantly, I went up the stairs, stopping on every step to listen, and with all my senses, not just with my ears. Nothing now would be strange to me; all inside me still lay in wait for something outrageously odd; for I knew that this night could not conclude without something wonderful happening: this sultriness couldn't end without lightning. Again, as I stood on the staircase landing and listened, I was the whole world outside, which strained in its helplessness and shrieked for a thunderstorm.

But nothing stirred. Only a mild breath moved through the motionless house. Tired, disappointed, I took the last step and stood with horror before my room, as if before a coffin.

The doorknob gleamed uncertainly in the dark. It was moist and warm to my touch. Behind it, the window opened out onto a black square of night, where the firs with their sharpened crests stood in the forest against a shred of clouded sky. It was dark outside and in, both world and room, only—this was odd and hard to explain—something slender stood in a forlorn strip of moonlight framed by the window. Stepping closer, I was amazed to see what glimmered so brightly there in the moon-veiled night, astonished to see it move, but I wasn't frightened, for something inside me tonight had strangely prepared itself for the incredible. Somehow I'd dreamed of it all beforehand. No encounter would have been strange to me, this one in the least, for it was *she* who stood there—she, whom I'd thought of unconsciously, with every step, every stride, in that sleeping house. It was she whose alertness my senses, incited, had felt through hall and door. I saw her face as only a glow, and her white nightgown lay round her like mist. She was leaning against the window, and, standing all elegant there against the landscape—mysteriously drawn from the shimmering mirror of the depths to her destiny—she looked really fabulous—like Ophelia over the pond.

I stepped closer, shy and excited both. The sound must have reached her; she turned. Her face was in the shadows. I can't say that she really looked at me or heard me, for there was nothing sudden in her movement—no fright and no resistance—and all around us was utterly still except for a little clock that ticked on the wall. Yes, all was very quiet till suddenly she said gently, without my expecting it:

"I'm so afraid."

She was speaking . . . to *me*? Did she mean *me*? Had she recognized *me*? Was she talking in her sleep? Hers was the same voice, the same quivering sound that had made me so shudder that afternoon when the clouds were coming and I'd not really taken much note of the look. This was strange, but I wasn't amazed or confused. I just stepped toward her to calm her and take her hand, which felt like tinder, hot and dry, while her fingers' grip seemed to crumble within my grasp.

Without a sound, she gave me her hand. Everything about her was limp, defenseless, and numb, except her lips, from which came a whisper, like something far off:

"I'm so afraid! I'm so afraid."

And then, in a dying sigh, like the last gasp of someone resigned to being smothered:

"Ah, how sultry it is!"

That sounded as if from far off, and yet was softly whispered, like a secret between us. Still, as I took hold of her arm, I felt she was not really speaking to *me*, for she just trembled gently, like trees in the afternoon before a thunderstorm, and when I grasped her more firmly, she didn't resist but just gave in. Weak, without resistance—a warm, plunging wave—that was how her shoulders fell against me. Now, with her right beside me, I could breathe the sensuousness of her hair and its damp mist. I didn't stir, and she remained silent.

All this was odd, and it sparked my curiosity, though by and by, I grew impatient. When I touched my lips to her hair, again, she didn't resist. When I took her lips, they were dry and hot, and, while I was kissing them, they suddenly opened to drink from mine, not from thirst and passion but with the silent, limp, and longing sucking of a child. "Someone dying of *thirst*," I thought to myself; and, as her lips sucked, her body—slender, warm, and heaving through the thin nightgown—absorbed me as earlier, outside, the *night* had: without any strength but full of a silent and drunken greed. And then, while I held her (my senses still gleamed piercingly, each to each), I felt the warm, moist *earth* on me as I had earlier: the hot and helpless and glowing landscape, thirsting for the release of tension, the shudder and shower of relaxation. I kissed and kissed her as if enjoying the great, sultry, waiting world in her, as if this warmth that glowed from her cheeks were the steam of the fields, as if the shuddering land breathed from those soft, warm breasts.

Yet then, as my lips meant to wander on up to her eyelids and then to her eyes (whose black flames I so felt); as I rose to look at her face (and in looking, more strongly to enjoy), I saw with surprise that her eyes were fast shut. A Greek mask of stone, eyeless, helpless, she lay there, Ophelia, dead and drifting on the waters now, the numb face rising palely from the dark flood.

I shuddered, feeling, for the very first time, the reality in all this. For I was taking a sleepwalker here—someone unconscious, drunk, or sick. Someone whose life I held in my arms, someone who didn't know what she was doing, who maybe did not even want me—someone this muggy night had just driven to me like a dangerous red moon. I got scared, and in my arms she was getting heavy. Gently I tried to let this passive creature glide on over to the easy chair or the bed, for I had no wish to steal pleasure from one in a fit of unconscious rapture. No, I wasn't about to take delight in something that maybe *she* did not want—something that maybe only some demon inside her, some devil lording it over her blood—desired.

But she hardly felt me easing up than she faintly started to beg and groan:

"Don't leave me! Don't leave me!"

41

And her lips sucked even more heatedly, and she pressed her body to mine. Eyes shut, her face was stretched painfully; and, shuddering, I felt that she wanted to wake and couldn't, that her drunken senses cried out from the prison of this derangement and wished for consciousness. Even under this leaden mask of sleep struggled something that longed for release from its bewitchment, and this dangerously lured me to rouse her. My nerves burned with impatience to see her awake, speaking as a real being and not just some wanderer in a dream. I wanted, at any cost, to force the truth from her silently savoring body.

So I yanked her to me. I shook her. I clamped my teeth in her lips. I dug my fingers into her arms to force her to open her eyes and consider, actively, what a mere dumb urge in her now enjoyed.

But she just bent and groaned under the painful embrace. "More! More!" she stammered, with an ardor, a senseless fervor, that excited me, made me senseless myself. And I felt that she was nearly awake, that consciousness soon would break out from beneath those shut eyelids, for she was already twitching restlessly, so I grabbed her more tightly, dug myself deeper into her, and at once felt a tear roll down her cheeks, which I drank like salt. Oh, terribly did it heave, her breast, the more I pressed her! How she groaned! How her limbs cramped, as if they wanted to force open something dreadful, enormous, a ripeness that closed around her with sleep, when suddenly—like lightning through the thundering world—it broke in two in her. Suddenly she was heavy again, a burdensome weight in my arms. Suddenly her lips let go of me; her hands sank; and as I leaned her back on the bed, she just lay there like someone dead.

I got scared again. By instinct I felt her—touched her arms and cheeks. She was really quite cold—chilled, stone-like—though in her sleep, her blood ticked gently, in trembling beats. A marble statue she was, lying there, cheeks moist with tears, her breath playing gently about her stretched nostrils. At times, a twitching, an ebbing wave of vexed blood, streamed over her; yet her breast heaved more and more gently. More and more, she seemed to become an image. More and more human and childlike, brighter and more relaxed, her limbs. The spasm had left her. She slumbered. She slept.

I kept sitting there on the edge of the bed, bent over her, quivering, while she just lay there, a peaceful child, eyes shut and mouth softly smiling, enlivened by a dream from within. Leaning quite close, I saw every line of her face singly; I felt the touch of her breath on my cheeks; and the more I focused my gaze on her, the more distant and secret she grew. Where was she now with her musings, she who lay there like stone, like someone dead spilled onto a beach, someone who'd drifted here from the heated current of a sultry night to me, a stranger? Who *was* this who lay here in my arms? From where had she come, to what had she listened? I knew nothing of her, and I felt that nothing bound her to me. Gazing at her for lonely minutes, while the clock only ticked overhead with zeal, I tried to read her speechless face, yet she confided nothing. I wished that she'd wake from this strange sleep beside me, here in my room, close to my life; yet I also felt, at the very same time, fear at the thought of her coming round, of her first waking glance.

So I sat there silent for maybe an hour or two, bent over the sleep of this stranger who by and by no longer seemed a woman, a human being who by some bizarre chance had entered my room, but the night itself. For the secret of tormented, longing nature had opened itself to me. Right here, below me, lay the whole hot world with her sweltering senses, it seemed—as if the earth had rebelled in her agony and sent her as herald from out of this strange, incredible night.

And now something rattled behind me. I started like a criminal. It was the window. It shook as if a tremendous fist were striking it. I sprang up. Before it stood something strange: a transformed night, new and dangerous, darkly gleaming and full of wild movement. A whistling, a terrible rustling rose from the sky's black tower, hurled itself toward me out of the night, cold and damp and with a wild thrust: the wind. It sprang from the dark, strong and forceful; hammered at the house; shook its fist at the window, which flew open like a frightful abyss. Clouds whirled up, erecting black walls in frenzied haste. Something whistled violently between sky and world. This wild current tore the persistent sultriness away; all flooded, stretched, and stirred; a frenzied flight traversed the sky; and, though rooted fast in the earth, the trees groaned beneath the unseen, piping whip of storm. And suddenly, this ripped wide in two: a crack of lightning, the sky splitting down to the ground. And behind it, the thunder roared as the clouds cracked in the lowlands.

Behind me too, something moved. She'd waked up. The lightning had torn the sleep from her eyes. She stared all around her, confused.

"What is it?" Where am I?" she said, her voice quite different from before. Fear still quivered within it, but the sound rang clear now, sharp and clean as the newborn air. Lightning flung open the frame of the landscape: the firs' contours, shaken by the storm, lit up in the air; the clouds ran over the sky like frenzied beasts; the room flashed chalk-white—even whiter than her face. She sprang up, her movements suddenly free, like someone totally different, and she stared at me in the darkness, her look seeming darker than the night.

"Who are you? . . . Where am I?" she stammered, clutching her opened nightgown over her breast in fright.

When I stepped nearer, to calm her, she only evaded me, screaming "What do you want with me?" as I approached her, and though I wished to find a word to calm her, to make an impression on her, I had to admit to myself, for the very first time, that I did not even know her name. Meanwhile, lightning flashed all over the room; the walls shone white as chalk, as if coated with phosphorus; and she stood there all white in front of me, her arms pressed against me in fright, her eyes now completely aware and her face now twisted in boundless hate. In vain I wished, while the thunder assaulted us there in the dark, to hold her, calm her, explain to her somehow; but—as a new flash of lightning revealed—she tore away, threw open the door, and dashed out.

And, with the shutting of the door, the thunder crashed down like all heaven fallen to earth.

Then it roared. Brooks plunged from infinite heights like waterfalls; the storm tossed them like wet ropes thrashing to and fro. At times it shot a clump of ice-cold water and sweet, spiced air inside the window frame, where I stood watching till my hair was wet and I dripped from the chill, chill showers. Yet I was blessed to feel the clean element; I too was casting my sultriness off in the midst of all the lightning; and I wanted to shout for joy. I forgot everything in my ecstasy; I could breathe and feel fresh again; and, like the earth, like the land, like the trees, I absorbed this coolness into me, felt the blessèd shower shake through my being, as did the trees, which swung hissing under the wet rods of rain. Demonically lovely, this voluptuous struggle of sky and earth: a gigantic wedding night whose delight I savored, shared. With lightning, the sky reached down; with thunder, it fell on all who trembled below; and there it was,

45

in this groaning darkness, a frenzied sinking into each other of high into low, of low into high, as in sex.

I watched as the trees now moaned with desire; as, with ever-glowing lightning, the expanses stitched themselves together; as the sky's heated veins stood open and flashed and mixed with the wet rivulets of paths; as everything, both night and world, broke apart and rushed together—a marvelous new kind of breathing wherein the fields' fragrance mingled with the sky's fiery breath and forced its chillness into me. Three weeks' detained heat was released in this battle, and I too felt an easing of tensions. The rain seemed to pour through my pores. The wind seemed to whistle all through my breast, rinsing it clean, and I felt that my self and existence were no longer alone, no longer dependent on other entities for their life; instead, I was, in the midst of nature's exuberance, just *World, Hurricane, Shower, Being,* and *Night.* And then, as all grew quieter by and by, the lightning now merely blue and harmlessly roaming along the horizon, the thunder rumbling only in fatherly warning, the roaring of the rain growing rhythmic within the exhausted wind, there came to me too, by and by, a certain softness and fatigue. My nerves vibrated like music; a gentle relaxing sank into my limbs.

O, to sleep with nature now, and then to awake with her! I threw my clothing off, myself into bed. Yes, soft, strange forms still lingered within. Yes, I vaguely felt her. Yes, the strange adventure would be recalled one more time. Yet I understood it no longer. Outside, the rain roared and roared and washed my thoughts away. It all seemed only a dream. I still wished to reflect on it, but the rain roared and roared and streamed through my thoughts till the night became a gentle, resounding cradle in which I sank, asleep within her own slumber.

The next morning, stepping up to the window, I saw a transformed world. Clear, with firm contours, the land lay cheerful in certain, resplendent sun; and higher above it, a radiant mirror of this stillness, curved the blue and distant horizon. Borders were clearly drawn; infinitely distant stood the sky that on the night before had burrowed deep in the fields and made them fertile. Now he was only far off—a world away and without connection; nowhere did he touch the fragrant, breathing, and silenced earth, his wife. A blue gulf shimmered coolly between him and the valley; without desire and as strangers, they stared at each other, landscape and sky.

I went down into the hall, where people had already gathered, their natures also changed from what they had been in those grim sultry weeks, for now everyone stirred and moved; their laughter rang brightly; their voices sounded melodic, metallic. The musty closeness that had hindered them so had dispersed; the sultry bond that had woven around them had been sloughed off. And I sat down among them without the slightest hostility, though a certain curiosity in me now sought the one whose image had almost stolen my sleep from me. And there, at a nearby table between her mother and father, she sat, the one I sought, cheerful, her shoulders light as she laughed resoundingly, free of care.

I seized her, questioning, with my stare. She didn't notice me. She was saying something that made her happy, and a childish laugh bubbled forth from the words. At last she looked at me; and with fleeting, fugitive touches, her laughter instinctively faltered. She eyed me again, more sharply. Something seemed to displease her; she pushed up her brows. Severely, sternly, her eyes surveyed me. By and by her face took on a strained tension, as if she were trying to remember something but couldn't. I stayed eye to eye with her, hoping a sign of shame or excitement would greet me.

But she'd looked away again. After a minute her look returned once more, to make sure. Once more it probed my face. For only a second—a long, drawn-out second—did I feel that hard and stinging metallic probe pierce deep into me. Then she calmly let her eyes drift away from me; and in the bright awkwardness of her glance—the light, almost happy turn of her head—I felt that, awake, she knew nothing more of me, that our sense of communion was lost with the magical darkness. We were as strange and distant again as sky and earth. She spoke to her parents, rocked her slender young shoulders without concern, and her teeth shone cheerfully in a smile between the slender lips from which, mere hours before, I had drunk the thirst and sultriness of a whole world.

LANDSCAPE

Night. And seeds, in slumber, breathe
Hot and sense-benumbing scents,
And silver mists arise and seethe:
Laments of an air still, sultry, tense.

Far off, the glare of a thunderstorm
Threatens on the horizon. *Soon* . . .
Clouds circle birds in a frightened swarm,
Along with the sallow, glowing moon.

And thunder groans as if in pain,
Beckons to the expectant land,
And strokes the ripe, rustling ears of grain
With sudden, ominous, silencing hand.

RADIANT NIGHT

The sky, whereon the shining stars now hover,
Has breathed and stretched itself far out, immense,
And night-enveloped flowers scatter over
The transformed land their warm and fragrant scents.

The woods now burn as blue as amethyst.
They do not stir. The trees stand, mere mute things.
And so much stillness—as if the land were kissed
Peremptorily, by angels' wings . . .

And every heart must feel this blessing, for
A dream will now take gently in its hand
All paths that stray and guide them to that door
That leads into the Promised Land.

LATE AUTUMN IN MERANO

By October's end, the last grapes have long since left the vine, but the vineyards still glow—with a soft yet fiery light. Leaf after leaf shines bright, the hue of brass; and always, whenever a gentle breeze makes them flutter and tilt, one thinks he hears them clink like fine metal discs. Autumn gazes more darkly into the land. The apples, with their red children's cheeks, glance only seldom through the brittle thicket; the chestnut trees shed their leaves more swiftly and violently; the last dark kernels are slung from their frosted hulls; yet winter still seems endlessly distant.

Though solemn November entered the valley days ago, the landscape smiles at him peacefully. Snow already cloaks the mountains' highest peaks, but their breasts still lie free and green, the vineyards' gaudy garter still laced shiningly round their high hips. Winter still seems quite far off. Only the heights, which gaze farther into the distance, seem to have spied him; the vale still frolics in the sun and waxes only fierier in its autumnal hues. Here and there, lone trees, like burning bushels, flicker their crimson warning into the land; their trunks glow the hue of rust; and the cheerful lemon of the withered leaves mingles gladly with the meadows' deep green. Above, the unchanging blue sky envelops, with a fully-stretched tone, the motley dance of varied hues. It is an autumn without end, without bitterness, which slowly becomes winter here and—one already feels it—a mild and restful one, without harshness or harm.

The play of varied colors in this landscape is not new to me. I've often seen it in the magic of transition like this, and I'm always gladdened and stirred, but always only as, for instance, a painter might see it, happy for the purity of the air and the blissful clarity of the colors and unquestionably given over to gentle joys. Yet today it gives me pleasure to inquire into the heart of this beauty, for there are times when pleasure and even happiness demands to be accounted for. I look into her cheerful features and ask my own heart, still glowing with delight, why this peculiar power to spread pure peacefulness into me and strew, from her own soft serenity, a reflection in me, has been given only to her. I know more powerful landscapes, crowned with the heroic insignias of grand pasts, landscapes which have the sea at their feet and find their graceful image established endlessly over some lake—landscapes like petrified primeval concepts, tragedians of wood and stone. I survey them, searching a hundred spots in the effort to grasp their beauty, and not a single thing replies. For nothing in them is really odd or unique; nothing imperiously draws one's gaze to it or intimately lets it flow from one line to the next.

And this harmony of transition is Merano's magic. For in her valley, all beauty's elements are not only distributed, but also combined. She has greatness and power, this landscape at the foot of the northern Alps, but one that does not oppress and weigh you down: if the mountains are shoved behind her threateningly, like angry wrinkles on some giant's brow; if one's view seems threatened on all sides by borders that warningly show the singular in the symbolic, then toward the south the sealed landscape opens up endlessly: a sunny vale that guides the eye along the freed and cheerfully fruitful fields. She is superb, this landscape, her nearby places lovely, her distant spots sublime. Her rocky structure does not frighten as does, say, a sealed mountain terrain, whose steep cliffs ultimately erect themselves around one's heart; her expanses do not tire, for they do not run level into the distance but are interlinked everywhere in a chain on the heights.

Everything in her vista is in transition. Even the city itself, ancient, yet tasteful with its pergolas and manor houses

52

and new villas and castles, places past and present side by side on convivial common ground. White, yet ever veined with green by its parks and grounds, it climbs slowly into the meadows and vineyards which, rising in turn, fade into the dark forest. This, in turn, is lost scrambling into the rock, whose grayness is gradually dusted over with the white of the firn, and this highest jagged line, in its turn, is etched into infinite blue. The fields of color unfold so cleanly and purely here that nothing clashes with anything else; all contrasts dissolve harmoniously. North and south, city and landscape, Germany and Italy—all these sharp oppositions glide into one another gently; and even the most antagonistic seem sociable, intimate here. Nowhere in the landscape is there a brusque movement, nowhere a torn or broken line; here, as if with a rounded, restful script, nature has inscribed the word *peace* into the earth.

Mastery of transition: that is the power of these southern Tirolean valleys. And not only in the structures of their own lives is the change in appearance vanquished, but also in the cycle of the seasons, for the very sky under which they rest seems tamed by their calming force. Yes, here the seasons, those four hostile sisters, are peacefully held in check: hand in hand, they softly turn in a round. They do not shove one another away in anger; they do not rob one another's places. Instead, they hand this world on, like a colorful ball, in cheerful play.

So I don't know whether to say that it's still autumn or already winter; one would almost think that the heights and the lowlands, the cliffs and the valley, are here made one, the way they both greet me at once as they do. For above, on the firn, snow already gleams; in wild gales, winter blasts through the firs, while below, the valley sparkles in sun-bathed air; a southern summer, an eternal youth, lifts its reflection to the gray cliffs. And in summer, by turns, when July seethes in the lowlands' overheated kettle, above us, on the Vigiljoch and the Mendel, a bright spring gleams through the almost winterishly chill and tangy air. This double world thus eases the excesses of the seasons through the neighborly presence of the others, and even on single days, in the span of a few hours, one may be able to find both here—winter in the morning and spring at noon—if the sun has drunk away the white hoarfrost and spread its friendly warmth over the valley. The seasons here are like siblings. As on an antique picture adorned with the colorful allegories of fruits, they change and achieve the friendly miracle of encountering one another, united.

Merano's landscape has achieved this wonder throughout, banning as it has that old disturber of the peace, the wind. For the wind alone is what forcefully separates the seasons, suddenly tearing their dance asunder. How often in the north has one experienced it in the night, when the windows rattled, when a howl—a moan of desperate resistance, a struggle and a cry— rushed along the street, and not until the next morning, when the snow lay white on the roofs, did one know that autumn had been abducted— whisked away in unseen chains—for one more long year. And just as powerfully does the storm hurl spring over winter and winter over autumn again. With one heave, he tears her yellow gown from the shivering trees and strews it into the distance; with one push, he flings the snow from the mountains so that the rivers foam up and roll, raging, into the valley. Whipped away in wild alarm, every season flees before him; one feels shocked and amazed in the face of the earth's new and unexpected countenance, then displeased before growing used to it.

But the landscape here, with her tall shoulders, resists his angry onslaught. The transition is not sudden, but imperceptibly tender, almost like music. Every day now, the sun extends its arc somewhat more narrowly; every night, the frost absorbs a drop of green blood from the trees. First the leaves start to yellow; then they rust to a brownish red; then they wither and shrivel, in order, at last, when they're quite weak and tired, to teeter sleepily away from the tree and sink in soft and circling descent to the earth. Yet they do not blow away: they merely sink faintly at one's feet and gently throng round the leaf-shorn trunk, as if this wilting foliage sought to warm the roots for the coming spring. And, as each single leaf does, so does the whole landscape here have its full play of colors, so that one feels the autumn and winter seasons not as shocks and surprises but calmly enjoys them as one might a play. Fruit after fruit falls, color on color gradually fades; but never does the snow settle, white and dead, between fading and blooming; and the new beginning ever draws close upon the time of dying away. But in the meantime, without tiring, the ivy everywhere holds his green vigil till spring, when the colors come again. Here there is no pause in the stimulating play of colors and light, only transition, a gently suggestive and gently ebbing harmony once again.

This is one secret of her beauty: her enmity with the wind. The second is her flourishing friendship with the sun. Merano lives by light, and one never feels this more strongly than on a rainy day, when suddenly all her cheerful features drown in tears, and clouds from afar come and veil her head. Her colors then shine only dully, as if through a screen; her people, with all their gaudy garb, hide themselves in their houses; the spirit of the hours is forfeited; and one finds his heartfelt connection to her beauty (which, only yesterday, was so close) no more.

For Merano lives only in light. Here the sun holds a strange, almost mythic power: she counts the hours; she structures the day; she nourishes the sick with hope, the fruits with her heated blood. When she first looks up, the day begins; when she sinks, it is past. With glowing compass, she measures the hours—more expansively in summer, more acutely in winter—but is ever orderly and exact; and each season gauges its time from her. After settling down in Merano a while, one can soon do without a watch, for the pink cloud on the mountain, which rushes ahead to announce her coming, proclaims that certain hour and moment when she reaches that church roof with her slanting ray, and then those when her light at last gleams down on the waters of the Passer. And so, in turn, when this house, then that, sinks in shadow; and by and by, every single point of the landscape is transformed by the count of a sundial on which one may see the rise and fall of the hours. The whole landscape, in fact, is one enormous sundial; and this visible regularity holds a miraculous attraction for all who have grown estranged from the sacred signs of the heavens' clock.

For we in the cities mainly trace morning and evening by the light of our rooms. We know that night is falling when the lines in our books melt away—when we must turn on a lamp and completely forget the giving power that all light stems from and that is ever so sensually ready for us there. Here, by contrast, the morning dawns only idly till the moment the sun feels her way down the mountains and into the valley. Only then does she, the world, awake; all at once people are out on the streets; music starts up on the promenades. And the gardens, too, where the light, with swift fingers, whisks away the damp frost, suddenly shine in a summerish way, as if they would once more bloom with flower and fruit. All is urged to this spot to drink in the sun; the whole town is transformed, as it were; the houses hold their balconies and terraces (on which, not unlike huge sunflowers, the round umbrellas watch over the sick) toward the south; the landscape's brightness doubles with every glance; and the last mists flee in the form of white clouds agleam in the sky. Only when the sun is awake, only so long as she bathes the valley with her warm waves, does the day last here. Golden spheres of light, grand and glowing in summer, faintly flashing and tiny in winter, roll these hours of sun from mountain to mountain, encircling all of life in manifold mirror images, tumbling it out of night and back into it. If the sun sinks behind a mountain, twilight falls as coolly and quickly as a fine gray shower of ash. Everything changes. The air, which, filtered through by the sun, felt soft and golden, suddenly grows chill as snow. The colors vanish, and so do the people. Here there is always a quarter hour, a half hour of fright, so to speak: a dive into the dark as sudden and shocking as when one looking out of a train compartment onto a lovely sunny landscape all at once feels snatched into a tunnel and stares, with a look of displeasure, into an unexpected night.

But the calming down begins as soon as the lights in the houses start to gleam, and, if one lives on the heights, it is indescribably lovely to see how a thousand sparks now glow throughout the deep vale. A ring of stars, they shimmer in the lowlands among the little moons of the electric lamps and, faintly gleaming in their midst, the foaming Passer. In the background, the starry sky holds, like a mirror, its image up to infinity; one world emulates the other; and above, on the mountains' rim, many a light on the summits already sparkles impudently toward eternity. Only now does one feel the inner severity in this landscape, whose serene and sunny gaze reveals, by day, only mildness; only now, in the ever deeper stillness, does one hear her speech in the plunging roar of the river. By day one saw only her smile; now one hears her heart.

This wonderful simultaneity of every contrast seems to be the endearing quality of the world of Merano, with which I, as a native by choice, feel a renewed bond over and over. One will never be successful (I feel this again and again in the attempt) in trying to explain her hospitable and accommodating beauty to someone who always seeks in beauty only what is worth *seeing*—the visibly spectacular, the priceless view—those notions of the hurried and ignorant, which from poverty of *in*sight have stamped landscapes and works into banknotes in the press of fame. Some cannot sense that one can form a friendship with a landscape, that one can hold a dialogue with her, that one can soften her hues on sheer sight and learn from the composure with which she meets reversals that are inevitable. Perhaps nothing can explain such a soothing influence, which often streams from the single line of a gently descending mountainside, from the ringing slopes of a beautifully-curved hill, right into the blood and forms, in further transformation, even friendlier resolutions and thoughts. Yet I believe that, unconsciously through the years, there is ultimately formed, in almost everyone, a special preference for a certain region that certainly signifies more than mere satisfaction with accommodations or climate. One feels that this landscape, which entices one with such steadfast insistence, holds its restless and flowing form ever in a firm (and because of that) not disorderly image; and one is pleased to see one's own fleeting existence fixed somewhere in its eternal form.

So I love this world of Merano with a longing that only heightens as the years go by. From her I have learned how to dissolve life's necessary conflict through harmony. Even here in the city, it is often soothing for me, the skyless and oppressed, to know that there down South, this life—in which, through love and devotion, I have left so much of myself—this life so cheerfully blooms again, as perhaps some inner urge in me, amid all the confusion and busyness, does. Far from her, I still feel her calm composure ring on in my blood; and when the city huddles together here under the fist of winter, and the stars are lost in fog, I sometimes take pains, for comfort's sake, to see her countenance within me, as it now, down south, in winter's gentle noon light and with snow on the firn, softly smiles and dreams of the coming spring.

CITY ON THE LAKE

Konstanz

Ever distant in sunset's radiance,
A German city in all its earnestness,
Its lines ensconced in clouds of such soft tints
As those that evenings in June alone possess.

Through dark leaves, from the lakeside park, escapes
A song. Don't you know that old song anymore?
As nice and cloudy as juice from turgid grapes,
It slowly flows across to us from the shore.

Your heart then yearns as if for home, and yet
Now sees the city for the first time, it seems—
Sees, for the very first time, its dark silhouette
Liquefy, mist-veiled, in the moon's pale beams.

SUNRISE IN VENICE

The bells awake. A shimmer, spark
Still quivering, faint, now flickers on
The canals; and, peeled from the dreaming dark,
The city's eternal lines are drawn.

Soft hues and chimes now fill the air.
Lagoons light up with silver ray.
Bellringers tug at ropes that flare
As if tearing into the world the day.

Now let the flood of dawn begin!
From drifting clouds, soft down's unrolled.
The clanging, hammering bells now spin
From tower to tower a web of gold.

And on and on! Ever faster it speeds.
Dawn swells, then billows, spilling its wine.
And sun streams forth like fire that feeds
Its greed on one, then the next roof line.

Dawn melts in gold flecks, piece by piece.
Every roof is glory agleam.
The restless bells now know release
And, in their beaming towers, dream.

SONG OF THE HERMIT

How strange a fate: to search, explore
The crazy maze of every road
And find it leads to this narrow door—
Yes, find I'm blessed with this bleak abode!

The silent stars, so pure and near,
Breathe on me their magic powers,
Banishing earthly joy, pain, fear
From all my mortal hours.

The sweet breath of my violin
Fills my room with serenity;
And so I turn toward evening; then
The voice of God will wake in me.

How strange a fate: to search, explore
The crazy maze of every road
And find it leads to this narrow door—
Yes, find I'm blessed with this bleak abode!

TWO MORNING SONGS

Bolzano

Now it tiptoes from the dark.
Locked and blind, the doors.
But then, from house to house, a spark
Of dawn light stretches, pours.

On morning's chill air seems to stream
The breath of coming things.
A flash of distant lands, a gleam,
Escapes the mist's frail wings.

And all feels great and clean to you
As Heaven on a holy day;
Devout words make their way to you,
And yet you need not kneel and pray;

Just bear your trembling heart with you
Into the listening day.

II

Ah, how, with bliss, I feel it still:
The breath of dawn upon my lips.
My thirsty, longing mouth now sips
Chill scents of blooms on field and hill.

Mountains shed mist's heavy gown,
While brooks as bright as nascent day
Mirror skies as clear as they
In waves that laugh and clatter down.

Though Sun's not in the valley yet,
One senses her proximity
As, spying far-off realms, I see,
Upon that ridge, her amulet.

Above the still quite mute expanse,
Shiningly, she hurls her lance
Inflamed with blood. Then the entire
Panorama glows with fire.

A church below us feels the blaze
Upon her roof. Her bells now stir
And wax with glad, enticing praise.
My heart rings out with her.

AUTUMN SONNET

The days have long since climbed down the golden ladder
Of summer. A waning brilliance warms the land.
The shadows wax much sooner, fall in sadder
Spans from every tree in evening's hand.

Many ripe fruits, wind-tossed and -oppressed,
Still gleam in the leaves. The meadow's breast is bare.
The clouds are chasing one other west
And make the sky seem restless, fraught with care.

Above the woods (leaf-stripped, with forlorn look),
The swallows swirl in flight, as in distress;
And all this warns: Prepare for autumn now.

Incline tomorrow toward the landscape's book,
Whose motley letters seem to wave and bow
As with life's loveliest word: transitoriness.

TOWARD HOME

For some time now, no gleam of light;
A sea of mist has sunk
Tower, house, roofs left and right.
We alone press onward, drunk
With lust for Venus, gold and bright,

Who leads us on our darkling way
In soft accompaniment.
Joy fills the heart toward end of day . . .
The end for which we sense we're meant
We go to meet as if at play.

ALPINE GLOW ON LAKE ZÜRICH

Who summoned this painting in the window frame,
This image gliding with the gold winds' swell?
It calls me peacefully. I know its name:
Autumn, and it means farewell.

The mountains, melting in the day to air,
Now glow so near, in particled light!
O here as ever one feels: to be aware
Is halfway to submit to fate and night.

And feels it good, more quietly now, to start
The vesper way down through the valley
Where autumn evenings settle in early

And, before it parts from all the houses
That spray fire westward from their windows,
See the summer sun once more in the heart.

A MEMORY

Winter now erects his walls of white;
The whole world beams with light glad and serene;
Our park alone's forlorn: shorn of delight
To hear no strangers' sounds invade the scene,

As if he thought of those fond days we spent
Together here in frothy summer mood,
So moving is his lone and mute lament
Amid this vast and sodden solitude.

LAST POEM

In gratitude for my sixtieth year

More gently drifts the hour's round
Above already graying hair;
Not till the cup's dregs does the ground
Appear so gold and clear and fair.

Foreboding of approaching night
Disturbs not—rather, soothes and saves!
For now one knows the pure delight
Of worldly sights one no more craves.

Not doubting now what one's achieved,
Not lamenting what one's missed,
At this age, one feels relieved
To train for the day he'll not exist.

Never does one's prospect shine
As bright as in the border's glow,
Nor is love of life so fine
As in the gloom of letting go.

AFTERWORD

When we view the life of Stefan Zweig, we see a cyclone of activity: the writing and translating of poetry; the composing of plays, biographies, letters, essays, reviews, stories, novellas, a published novel and novel fragments, a libretto; travels all over Europe, to India, and to North and South America; friendships with a host of other famous figures (Auguste Rodin, Sigmund Freud, Arturo Toscanini, Rainer Maria Rilke, Romain Rolland, Hermann Hesse, and Richard Strauss, to name just a few); countless lectures and readings; two marriages; numerous affairs; and the enthusiastic collecting of literary manuscripts and memorabilia. In a little over sixty years, he accomplished the work of several lifetimes.

It is passion that marks his life and work, and the poems in this volume reflect it. Some, such as "Hymn for the Journey," show his love for travel and seeking new places; others, such as "Landscape," reveal a self-effacing immersion in the forces of nature. Even "Sunrise in Venice," though set in a city, displays Zweig's excitement when moved by nature's power to sanctify the world of man; and as such, like Wordsworth's "Composed Upon Westminster Bridge, September 3, 1802," it paints a mood of blissful solitude and union with nature in all her beauty.

Passion also pervades *A Girl and the Weather*, which first appeared in its original form as *Die Frau und die Landschaft* in 1922 and which has been issued by Fischer Verlag several times since then, most recently in 2001 as one of Zweig's

Meisternovellen (master novellas). In setting and theme, this piece resembles other tales by Zweig with which English audiences are familiar. Here, as in *Brennendes Geheimnis* (*Burning Secret*) and *Sommernovellette* (offered in English as *The Fowler Snared*), an Alpine resort provides the scene for lustful intrigue. In the first of these, a married woman on holiday with her son is nearly seduced by a lecherous young baron; in the second, an older man preys upon a young girl, stoking a longing for love in her by sending her unsigned love letters. In *A Girl with the Weather,* to be sure, we find another predatory male, though the satisfaction he seeks is quite direct, if yet again for a mere girl. What most distinguishes this tale from the other two, perhaps, is that its voice is that of the predator himself, unfiltered by the author's, as in *Burning Secret*, or the objective narrator's of *The Fowler Snared*. Absent is the tender ending of the first, in which the mother retains her virtue and is reunited with her son; absent, too, is the humbling of the old would-be lover in the second piece by the narrator, who attends to the older man's tale and calls into question his motives. Here, by contrast, there is no chastening effect, no hint of a moral authority underpinning the piece. The narrator here feels no regret, harbors no remorse for his lustful urges, makes no attempt to apologize. His spell is snapped when the drought ends; he falls asleep blissfully to the sound of the rain; he wakes, refreshed and renewed, the next morning. The ending is wholly amoral. The predator goes unpunished. The implication is that, overwhelmed by the powers of nature, he falls prey to his own instincts. Neither he nor the author offers excuses or begs forgiveness for the awakening of the primitive in him.

Primitive feeling also informs Zweig's lyrics, especially "Begehren" (here, "Desire") with its candid expression of lust, or "Blühen" ("In Bloom"), which revels in youthful feminine beauty with unabashed sensuality. We cannot help recalling Zweig's flings with young female admirers, as well as the fact that he translated Baudelaire. For a full understanding of the man, then, we cannot ignore his lyrics. They also shed light on the temperament of the narrator of *Die Frau und die Landschaft*. Even so, in their tenderness, they are far removed, say, from the cruelly manipulative husband of *Angst (Fear)* or the callous novelist of *Brief einer Unbekannten (Letter from an Unknown Woman)*, and we must bear in mind that Zweig's portrayals of women in his fiction are chiefly sensitive and sympathetic.

A Romantic longing for childhood also softens Zweig's passion at times. The man of *A Girl and the Weather* seems only too happy to slough off his sexual longings and drift off to sleep as the boy Edgar does at the end of *Burning Secret*. And, for all its admission of lust, "Desire" concludes with a wish on the author's part to return to days less harried by manly cravings.

Still other poems—with their more wistful, less wildly-excited responses to the natural world—show yet another side of Zweig. This was the Zweig who often rued his hectic public life and longed for another, quieter one. We see this Zweig in "The Hermit," who seeks refuge in bucolic solitude. We also find him in the 1913 travel piece "Late Autumn in Merano" ("Herbstwinter in Meran"), wherein, like Wordsworth in "Tintern Abbey," he shows us that landscapes can be imprinted upon our souls and so can give us sustenance during the years when we are apart from them. This is a Zweig, who, as Wordsworth relates in his preface to *Lyrical Ballads* (1802), knows that "the human mind is capable of being excited without the application of gross and violent stimulants."

And this is the Zweig to whom we should probably listen most. Perhaps the figure of Stefan Zweig appeals to our day so much because the frenzied pace of his life was one we all share; perhaps his sensational stories present for us—in all our malaise as slaves of machines and routine in a world conveniently insulated and almost wholly divorced from the life of nature—a passion and drama we crave. Perhaps we have so lost any connection to the earth that we hardly know what it *is* we lack. In any event, along with the voice of the dazzling fiction, we would do well to heed the quieter voice of the poems and essays in this book.

William Ruleman

ABOUT THE TRANSLATOR

William Ruleman grew up in Memphis, Tennessee, attended the University of the South at Sewanee, and received his bachelor's and master's degrees in English at the Universities of Virginia and Memphis, respectively. He went on to earn the Ph.D. in English in 1994 from the University of Mississippi. Thereafter, he taught literature and writing at Tennessee Wesleyan University until his retirement in 2018.

His other books of translation include two additional works by Stefan Zweig (*Vienna Spring: Early Novellas and Stories* and *Clarissa: the fragment of a novel,* both from Ariadne Press), as well as *Verse for the Journey: Poems on the Wandering Life* by the German Romantics, *Selected Poems* of Maria Luise Weissmann, and *Early Poems* of Hermann Hesse, all from Cedar Springs Books.

Volumes of his own poetry include *From Rage to Hope* (White Violet Books), *A Palpable Presence* and *Sacred and Profane Loves* (both from Feather Books), and, from Cedar Springs Books, *Munich Poems* and *Salzkammergut Poems.*